The Wonderful World of Boys

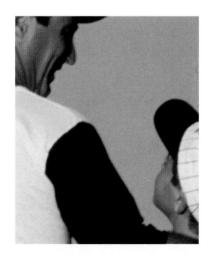

the Wonderful World
of BOYS

Photography by John C. Russell and Carl Yarbrough

DR. JAMES DOBSON

Tyndale House Publishers, Inc.
Wheaton, Illinois

Visit Tyndale's exciting Web site at www.tyndale.com

Cover and inside photographs by John Russell and Carl Yarbrough. All rights reserved.

This book contains material adapted from best-selling books by Dr. James Dobson: *Bringing Up Boys,* published in 2001 by Tyndale House Publishers; *Complete Marriage and Family Home Reference Guide,* published in 2000 by Tyndale House Publishers; *The New Dare to Discipline,* published in 1970, 1992 by Tyndale House Publishers; and *The Strong-Willed Child,* published in 1987 by Tyndale House Publishers.

Designed by Jackie Noe

Foreword by Peb Jackson

Library of Congress Cataloging-in-Publication Data

Dobson, James C., date.
    p. cm.
  ISBN 0-8423-8107-4 (HC)
   1. Parenting—Religious Aspects—Christianity. 2. Boys—Religious life.
I. Title.
BV4529 .D634 2003
248.8'45—dc21

Printed in Italy

08 07 06 05 04 03
8 7 6 5 4 3 2 1

2002014253

Table of Contents

Foreword

IT HAS BEEN MY GOOD FORTUNE to have a longtime friendship with the three guys who collaborated on this book. Jim Dobson and I started playing tennis together in the late 1970s, and I'm still smarting from the fact that he always beat me in singles—even with less talent. Carl Yarbrough and John Russell were working together in Aspen when I first met them in the mid-1980s. Subsequently my wife, Sharon, and I have been touched deeply by each of these friends and their families.

I had the good fortune to work with Jim Dobson for over thirteen years. He even participated in several Adventures in Fatherhood mountaineering courses I helped start, and he still gets sweaty palms thinking about rappelling off a one-hundred-foot cliff. He had to act heroic, of course, as his eleven-year-old son, Ryan, bounded down the face of the cliff with no fear at all.

It was during these adventures that I started my own fathering of boys who had lost their real fathers. Somehow the Lord allowed me to experience a bit of the essence of fatherhood, even though Sharon and I never had any children ourselves. However, over the last thirty-two years, Sharon has had to put up with the "oldest living adolescent."

My own father, Dr. Sheldon G. Jackson, once observed that my twin brother, Shel, and I repeatedly tested my mother's and his will and endurance, but he also said he wouldn't trade the experience of fatherhood for anything. That sentiment, I'm sure, is echoed by millions.

Since the mid-1980s, when John, Carl, and their families came into our lives, I've been trying to figure out how to get them to do a book of their photos. We've been fans and admirers of these world-class photographers for years, and now the dream is finally a reality. If you stopped by our home, you'd find large photos taken by these two men gracing our walls.

I love these guys, and I'm honored to link up with them and Tyndale in helping produce this timeless book. I trust that it will inspire you, the reader, to reach back and embrace your own memories and perhaps redouble your efforts with the boys in your sphere of influence. And if you still have boys in your care, I hope this book will help you to create your own images and memories that will bless you for the rest of your life.

PEB JACKSON
Colorado Springs, CO

Introduction

IT'S NO SECRET THAT BOYS AND GIRLS ARE DIFFERENT in ways
that may never be fully understood. If you're the parent of a boy, you know all too well just
how strong these differences are.

So what does this mean? Is masculinity good or bad, right or wrong? At first blush, it would
appear that girls have all the right stuff. On average, they make fewer mistakes, take fewer
risks, are better students, are more thoughtful of others, and are less impulsive than boys.
Was testosterone one of God's great mistakes? Would it be better if boys were more like
girls, and if men were more like women? Most certainly not. The sexes were carefully
designed by the Creator to balance each other's weaknesses and meet one another's needs.
Each sex has a unique purpose in the grand scheme of things.

How incredibly creative it is of God to give each gender different characteristics so that
there is a balance between the two. When they come together in marriage to form what the
Scripture calls "one flesh," they complement and supplement each other. Wouldn't it be
boring if men and women were identical? It just ain't so, and thank goodness it isn't.

As the father of one son myself, I know that a little boy's antics and sheer physicality are
bound to try our patience and sometimes even bring us to the brink of exhaustion. But in
the end, I've found that having a son has been one of the greatest joys in my life. A boy's
positive energy is exciting, and his happiness and humor are often contagious.

As you read through these pages and look at the classic photographs, I hope you'll be
reminded of the exuberance and richness boys bring to each day. Inside you'll find some
practical suggestions and encouragement to help you in your task of raising the next generation of men. You'll also be inspired to take a step back and appreciate the many lessons we
can learn from the boys in our lives: lessons about hope, understanding, creativity, kindness,
and love.

James Dobson

That Little Boy of Mine

Two eyes that shine so bright,

Two lips that kiss goodnite,

Two arms that hold me tight,

That little boy of mine.

No one could ever know
how much your coming has meant.
To me you're everything.
You're something heaven has sent.

You're all the world to me.

You climb upon my knee.

To me you'll always be

That little boy of mine.[1]

The Wonderful World of Boys

 GREETINGS TO ALL the men and women out there who are blessed to be called parents. There is no greater privilege in living than bringing a tiny new human being into the world and then trying to raise him or her properly during the next eighteen years. Doing that job right requires all the intelligence, wisdom, and determination you will be able to muster from day to day. And for parents whose family includes one or more boys, the greatest challenge may be just keeping them alive through childhood and adolescence.

We have a delightful four-year-old youngster in our family named Jeffrey who is "all boy." One day last week, his parents and grandparents were talking in the family room when they realized that the child hadn't been seen in the past few minutes. They quickly searched from room to room, but he was nowhere to be found. Four adults scurried throughout the neighborhood calling, "Jeffrey? Jeffrey!" No answer. The kid had simply disappeared. Panic

5

gripped the family as terrible possibilities loomed before them. Had he been kidnapped? Did he wander away? Was he in mortal danger? Everyone muttered a prayer while running from place to place. After about fifteen minutes of sheer terror, someone suggested they call 911. As they reentered the house, the boy jumped out and said, "Hey!" to his grandfather. Little Jeffrey, bless his heart, had been hiding under the bed while chaos swirled around him. It was his idea of a joke. He honestly thought everyone else would think it was funny too. He was shocked to learn that four big people were very angry at him.

Jeffrey is not a bad or rebellious kid. He is just a boy. And in case you haven't noticed, boys are different from girls. Haven't you heard your parents and grandparents say with a smile, "Girls are made out of sugar and spice and everything nice, but boys are made of snakes and snails and puppy-dog tails"? It was said tongue-in-cheek, but people of all ages thought it was based on fact. "Boys will be boys," they said knowingly. They were right.

ONE OF THE SCARIEST ASPECTS OF RAISING BOYS IS THEIR TENDENCY TO RISK LIFE AND LIMB FOR NO GOOD REASON.

One of the scariest aspects of raising boys is their tendency to risk life and limb for no good reason. It begins very early. If a toddler can climb on it,

he will jump off it. He careens out of control toward tables, tubs, pools, steps, trees, and streets. He will eat anything but food and loves to play in the toilet. He makes "guns" out of cucumbers or toothbrushes and likes digging around in drawers, pill bottles, and Mom's purse. And just hope he doesn't get his grubby little hands on a tube of lipstick. A boy harasses grumpy dogs and picks up kitties by their ears. His mom has to watch him every minute to keep him from killing himself. He loves to throw rocks, play with fire, and

shatter glass. He also gets great pleasure out of irritating his brothers and sisters, his mother, his teachers, and other children. As he gets older, he is drawn to everything dangerous—skateboards, rock climbing, hang gliding, motorcycles, and mountain bikes. At about sixteen, he and his buddies begin driving around town like kamikaze pilots on *sake.* It's a wonder any of them survive.

Our son, Ryan, encountered one dangerous situation after another as a boy. By the time he was six, he was personally acquainted with many of the local emergency room attendants and doctors. And why not? He had been their patient repeatedly. One day when he was about four, he was running through the backyard with his eyes closed and fell into a decorative metal "plant." One of the steel rods stuck him in the right eyebrow and exposed the bone underneath. He came staggering through the back door bathed in blood, a memory that still gives Shirley nightmares. Off they went to the trauma center—again. It could have been much worse, of course. If the trajectory of Ryan's fall had been different by as much as a half inch, the rod would have hit him in the eye and gone straight to his brain. We have thanked God many times for the near misses.

WE HAVE THANKED GOD MANY TIMES FOR THE NEAR MISSES.

I was also one of those kids who lived on the edge of disaster. When I was about ten, I was very impressed by the way Tarzan could swing through the trees from vine to vine. No one ever told me, "Don't try this at home." I climbed high into a pear tree one day and tied a rope to a small limb. Then I positioned myself for a journey to the next tree. Unfortunately, I made a small but highly significant miscalculation. The rope was longer than the distance from the limb to the ground. I kept thinking all the way down that something didn't seem right. I was still gripping the rope when I landed

flat on my back twelve feet below and knocked all the air out of the state of Oklahoma. I couldn't breathe for what seemed like an hour (it must have been about ten seconds) and was sure I was dying. Two teeth were broken and a loud gonging sound echoed in my head. But later that afternoon, I was up and running again. No big deal.

The next year, I was given a chemistry set for Christmas. It contained no explosives or toxic materials, but in my hands, anything could be hazardous.

LET LOVE BE YOUR GUIDE

A child should not be punished for behavior that is not willfully defiant. When he forgets to feed the dog or make his bed or take out the trash—when he leaves your tennis racket outside in the rain or loses his bicycle—remember that these behaviors are typical of childhood. It is, more than likely, the mechanism by which an immature mind is protected from adult anxieties and pressures. Be gentle as you teach him to do better. If he fails to respond to your patient instruction, it then becomes appropriate to administer some well-defined consequences (he may have to work to pay for the item he lost or be deprived of its use, etc.). However, childish irresponsibility is very different from willful defiance and should be handled more patiently.

After a time of conflict during which the parent has demonstrated his right to lead (particularly if it resulted in tears for the child), the youngster between two and seven (or older) may want to be loved and reassured. By all means, open your arms and let him come! Hold him close and tell him of your love. Rock him gently and let him know, again, why he was punished and how he can avoid the trouble next time. This moment of communication builds love, fidelity, and family unity. And for the Christian family, it is extremely important to pray with the child at that time, admitting to God that we have *all* sinned and no one is perfect. Divine forgiveness is a marvelous experience, even for a very young child.

Avoid impossible demands. Be absolutely sure that your child is *capable* of delivering what you require. Never punish him for wetting the bed involuntarily or for not becoming potty-trained by one year of age or for doing poorly in school when he is incapable of academic success. These impossible demands put the child in an unresolvable conflict: There is no way out. That condition brings inevitable damage to the human emotional apparatus.

Let love be your guide. A relationship that is characterized by genuine love and affection is likely to be a healthy one, even though some parental mistakes and errors are inevitable.[1]

[1]Dr. James Dobson, *The Strong-Willed Child* (Wheaton, Ill.: Tyndale House Publishers, 1987), 31–33.

I mixed some bright blue chemicals in a test tube and corked it tightly.

Then I began heating the substance with a Bunsen burner. Very soon, the

entire thing exploded. My parents had just finished painting the ceiling of

my room a stark white. It was soon decorated with the most beautiful blue

stuff, which remained splattered there for years. Such was life in the Dobson

household.

It must be a genetic thing. I'm told my father was also a terror in his time.

When he was a small boy, a friend dared him to crawl through a block-long

drainpipe. He could only see a pinpoint of light at the other end, but he

began inching his way into the darkness. Inevitably, I suppose, he became stuck somewhere in the middle. Claustrophobia swept over him as he struggled vainly to move. There he was, utterly alone and stranded in the pitchblack pipe. Even if adults had known about his predicament, they couldn't have reached him. Rescue workers would have had to dig up the entire pipe to locate and get him out. The boy who was to become my dad finally made it to the other end of the drain and survived, thankfully, to live another day.

Two more illustrations: My father and all of his four brothers were high-risk kids. The two eldest were twins. When they were only three years old, my grandmother was shelling beans for the night meal. "DON'T LET THE KIDS PUT THOSE BEANS UP THEIR NOSES." As my grandfather left for work, he said within hearing distance of the children, "Don't let the kids put those beans up their noses." Bad advice! As soon as their mom's back was turned, they stuffed their nasal passages with beans. It was impossible for my grandmother to get them out, so she just left them there. A few days later, the beans began to sprout. Little green shoots were actually growing out their nostrils. A family doctor worked diligently to dig out the tiny plants one piece at a time.

And years later, the five boys stood looking at an impressive steeple on a church. One of them dared the others to climb the outer side and see if they could touch the very highest point. All four of them headed up the structure like monkeys. My father told me that it was nothing but the grace of God that prevented them from tumbling from the heights. It was just a normal day in the life of five rambunctious little boys.

Parents need to "play offense"—to capitalize on the impressionable years of childhood by instilling in their sons the antecedents of character. Their assignment during two brief decades will be to transform their boys from immature and flighty youngsters into honest, caring men who will be respectful of women, loyal and faithful in marriage, keepers of commitments, strong and decisive leaders, good workers, and secure in their masculinity. And of course, the ultimate goal for people of faith is to give each child an understanding of Scripture and a lifelong passion for Jesus Christ. This is, I believe, *the* most important responsibility for those of us who have been entrusted with the care and nurturance of children.

Vive la Différence

ONE OF THE MOST ENJOYABLE aspects of my responsibility at Focus on the Family is to review the letters, telephone calls, and e-mails that flood into our offices. One of the most treasured came from a nine-year-old girl named Elizabeth Christine Hays, who sent me her picture and a list she had composed about girls and boys.

Dear James Dopson,

I hope you like my list of girls are better than boys. You are a good guy. I am a Christian. I love Jesus.

> *Love,*

> *Elizabeth Christine Hays*

P.S. Please don't throw my list away.

GIRLS ARE MORE BETTER THAN BOYS

1. Girls chew with their mouths closed.

2. Girls have better hand writing.

3. Girls sing better.

4. Girls are more talented.

5. Girls can do their hair better.

6. Girls cover their mouths when they sneeze.

7. Girls don't pick their nose.

8. Girls go to the bathroom politely.

9. Girls learn faster.

10. Girls are more kinder to animals.

11. Girls don't smell as bad.

12. Girls are more smarter.

13. Girls get more things what they want.

14. Girls don't let stinkers as much.

15. Girls are more quieter.

16. Girls don't get as durty.

17. Girls are cleaner.

18. Girls are more attractive.

19. Girls don't each as much.

20. Girls walk more politely.

21. Girls aren't as strict.

22. Girls sit more politely.

23. Girls are more creative.

24. Girls look better than boys.

25. Girls comb their hair better.

26. Girls shave more.

27. Girls put on deoderant on more often.

28. Girls don't have as much bodyodor.

29. Girls don't want their hair messed up.

30. Girls like to get more tan.

31. Girls have more manners.

I was so amused by Elizabeth Christine's creativity that I included her list in my next monthly letter and mailed it to approximately 2.3 million people. In my next monthly letter, I invited boys to send me their written opinions of girls. Here are selected items from the many lists that I received in the next couple of weeks.

WHY BOYS ARE MORE BETTER THAN GIRLS

1. Boys can sit in front of a scary movie and not close their eyes once.
2. Boys don't have to sit down every time they go.
3. Boys don't get embarrassed easily.
4. Boys can go to the bathroom in the woods.
5. Boys can climb trees better.
6. Boys can hang on to their stomachs on fast rides.
7. Boys don't worry about "diet-this" and "diet-that."
8. Boys are better tractor drivers than girls.
9. Boys rite better than girls.
10. Boys can build better forts than girls.
11. Boys can take pain better than girls.
12. Boys are way more cooler.
13. Boys have less fits.
14. Boys don't waste their life at the mall.
15. Boys aren't afraid of reptiels.
16. Boys shave more than girls.
17. Boys don't do all those wiggaly movmets when they walk.
18. Boys don't scratch.
19. Boys don't brade another's hair.

20. Boys aren't smart alickes.

21. Boys don't cry and feel sorry when they kill a fly.

22. Boys don't use as mutch deoderent.

23. Boys were created first.

24. Boys learn to make funny noises with their armpits faster.

25. Boys can tie better knots—specially girls pony tails.

26. Boys get to blow up more stuff.

27. Without boys there would be no babies. [Now there's a new thought!]

28. Boys eat with a lot of heart.

29. Boys don't WINE.

30. Boys hum best.

31. Boys are proud of their odor.

32. Boys don't cry over a broken nail.

33. Boys don't need to ask for directions.

34. Boys can spell Dr. Dobson's name correctly.

35. Boys aren't clichish.

36. Boys don't hog the phone.

37. Boys aren't shopacholics.

38. Boys bait their own hook when they fish.

39. Boys don't hang panty hose all over the bathroom.

40. Boys don't wake up with bad hair.

41. Boys aren't stinker. [what?]

42. Boys don't take two million years to get ready.

43. Boys couldn't care less about Barby.

44. Boys don't have to have 21 pairs of shoes (three for every day of the week!!!).

45. Boys don't put a tub of makeup on all the time.

46. Boys don't care if their noses aren't perfect.

47. Boys respect everything and everyone including GIRLS!

In addition to receiving many of these "more better" lists, I was sent some delightful notes from children written in their own handwriting. Obviously, the

debate about boys and girls had sparked some animated discussions in families all across North America. Here are a few examples from our mail:

I really like the page about "girls are more better than boys." I fond it because I was walking by the table and the word "girl" caught my eye. I believe every word on that piece of paper. I have been trying to convince my friend, Lenny, that girls are better than boys, now I have proof. NO OFENSE! Thank you for not throwing it away and for publishing it. I am eight, almost nine years old. —Faith, age 8

Most boys really don't care about the list Elizabeth made. Boys care more about sports, having fun, and not caring about the way they look (unless they are going somewhere nice). I was made to write this letter. Most boys do not like to write. —Michael, age 12

Elizabeth hasn't got a clue. —Anthony, age 8

We got your letter today with the list that was called, "Girls Are More Better Than Boys." I didn't think it was all true. I just thought some of it was true because my brother does his hair better than mine. —Stephanie, age 9

I really enjoyed reading Elizabeth Christine Hays' letter to you. I especially enjoyed her 31 reasons why girls are better than boys. My parents had me read these reasons to my brothers. The two oldest boys laughed through the whole thing. It was plain they didn't agree. But when I was done, my four-year-old brother said, "So girls are better than boys." —Sarah, age 15

I am eight years old. I read the letter that Elizabeth Hays wrote about girls being better than boys. I don't think anything on that list is true. I have two brothers that are just as special as I am. There is a verse in the Bible that says, "For the Lord does not see as man sees; for man looks at the outward appearance, but the Lord looks at the heart" (1 Samuel 16:7, NKJV). We should all try to look at other people the way the Lord looks at us. —Elisha, age 8

I was reading throu [your letter] and I saw the list of thirty-one reasons girls are better than boys. Know what I did with it? I stomped on it! your friend, Peyton. [no age given] P.S. you have permission to print this.

Don't you love the spontaneity and creativity of children? Boys and girls have such a fresh take on almost everything, and as we have seen, they view life from opposite ends of the universe. Even a child can see that boys and girls are different.

Scripture tells us, "God created man in his own image, in the image of God he created him; male and female he created them" (Genesis 1:27). Jesus, who was the first Jewish leader to give dignity and status to women, said, "Haven't you read . . . that at the beginning the Creator 'made them male and female,'" and "For this reason a man will leave his father and mother and be united to his wife, and the two will become one flesh" (Matthew 19:4-5). That is the divine plan. It leaves no doubt that the Creator made not one sex but two, each beautifully crafted to "fit with" and meet the needs of the other.

Fathers and Sons

 WHEN I WAS SEVENTEEN years old, the state of Texas granted me a license to drive. It was a bad decision. My dad had recently bought a brand-new Ford, and he let me take it out for a spin during lunchtime one day. That was another big mistake. Hundreds of my fellow students were milling around my school as I drove by, which gave me a great opportunity to show off. I also wanted to test a theory that had intrigued me. In our little town, there were huge dips on both sides of certain intersections to handle the flash floods that occasionally swept down our streets. I reasoned that if I hit the bumps at high speed, my car would sail over them. I was a big fan of Joey Chitwood, who was the Evel Knievel of that day, and I had seen him catapult his car over obstacles at the state fair. If Joey could do it, . . . why not me?

Obviously, there was much that I didn't understand about the physics of three thousand pounds of steel hurtling down the road. I approached the intersection helter-skelter and careened into the first dip. There was a violent reaction. *Kaboom!* went the bottom of the car! Then I blasted into the second canyon. *Kabang!* My head hit the headliner and the car convulsed up and down like a gigantic yo-yo. My entire life passed in front of my eyes. But my Texas friends were awestruck. In their Texas drawl, they said, "Wow! Look at tha-yet. He got ar under his tars."

A few weeks later, my good ol' dad came to me and said, "Uh, Bo," (that's what he called me) "I just took the car to the mechanic, and he said all four shocks have blown out. It's the craziest thing. Shocks usually wear out little by little, but the car is new and they're already shredded. Do you have any idea how this could have happened?"

> MY ENTIRE LIFE PASSED IN FRONT OF MY EYES. BUT MY TEXAS FRIENDS WERE AWESTRUCK.

The only thing that saved me was a momentary lapse of memory. At that second, I honestly didn't recall that I had hit the bumps, so I said no! He accepted my denial and I escaped with my life. A few weeks later, I was driving near our home when the steering column broke, sending the Ford into the curb. Fortunately, no one was killed. It was years later before I realized that I had blown the shocks and probably cracked the steering post during "the great physics experiment." Who knows what other damage I did to Dad's new car on that day.

ADVENTURES IN EATING

The dinner table is one potential battlefield where a parent can easily get ambushed. You can't win there! A strong-willed child is like a good military general who constantly seeks an advantageous place to take on the enemy. He need look no farther than the dinner table. Of all the common points of conflict between generations—bedtime, hair, clothes, schoolwork, etc.—the advantages in a food fight are all in the child's favor! Three times a day, a very tiny youngster can simply refuse to open his mouth. No amount of coercion can make him eat what he doesn't want to eat.

I remember one three-year-old who was determined not to eat his green peas, despite the insistence of his father that the squishy little vegetables were going down. It was a classic confrontation between the irresistible force and an immovable object. Neither would yield. After an hour of haranguing, threatening, cajoling, and sweating, the father had not achieved his goal. The tearful toddler sat with a forkload of peas pointed ominously at his sealed lips.

Finally, through sheer intimidation, the dad managed to get one bite of peas in place. But the lad wouldn't swallow them. I don't know everything that went on afterward, but the mother told me they had no choice but to put the child to bed with the peas still in his mouth. They were amazed at the strength of his will.

The next morning, the mother found a little pile of mushy peas where they had been expelled at the foot of the bed! Score one for Junior, none for Dad. Tell me in what other arena a thirty-pound child could whip a grown man!

Not every toddler is this tough, of course. But many of them will gladly do battle over food. It is their ideal power game. Talk to any experienced parent or grandparent and he or she will tell you this is true. The sad thing is that these conflicts are unnecessary. Children will eat as much as they need if you keep them from indulging in the wrong stuff. They will not starve. I promise![1]

[1] Dr. James Dobson, *Complete Marriage and Family Home Reference Guide* (Wheaton, Ill.: Tyndale House Publishers, 2000), 41.

By the time I admitted to myself that I was the guilty party, the statute of limitations had expired on my crime. My dad had forgotten about the episode and he never mentioned it again. Nor did I. My father went to his grave unaware of the stupid thing I had done. So Dad, if you're watching from up there, just know that I'm sorry and I won't ever do it again. I'll save my allowance for six years to pay for the damage. It was the only time I ever got "ar under my tars."

Boys have a way of frustrating and irritating the very souls of us dads. They leave our best tools out in the rain or they scramble them on the work-bench. They lose our binoculars and they drop our cameras. Many of them are sassy, irresponsible, and hard to handle. Or they do things that make absolutely no sense to the rational mind, such as little Jeffrey hiding under the bed while his family ran through the neighborhood shouting his name. Of course, we fathers shouldn't complain. We were boys once who drove our own dads crazy too, so we should cut our sons some slack. Despite all the challenges associated with raising a rambunctious kid, one of the greatest privileges in living is to have one of them hug your neck and say, "I love you, Dad."

BOYS HAVE A WAY OF FRUSTRATING AND IRRITATING THE VERY SOULS OF US DADS.

We as parents are raising the next generation of men who will either lead with honor and integrity or abandon every good thing they have inherited. They are the bridges to the future. We must make the necessary investment to build within our boys lasting qualities of character, self-discipline, respect for authority, commitment to the truth, a belief in the work ethic, and an unshakable love for Jesus Christ. It has been said, "No man stands so tall as when he stoops to help a boy." Another wise observer said, "Tie a boy to the right man and he almost never goes wrong." They are both right. When

asked who their heroes are, the majority of boys who are fortunate enough to have a father will say, "It's my dad." Boys are constructed emotionally to be dependent on dads in ways that were not understood until recently.

We now know that there are two critical periods during childhood when boys are particularly vulnerable. The most obvious occurs at the onset of puberty, when members of both sexes experience an emotional and hormonal upheaval. Boys and girls at that time desperately need their father's supervision, guidance, and love. But according to Dr. Carol Gilligan, professor at Harvard University, there is another critical period earlier in life—one not shared by girls. Very young boys bask in their mothers' femininity and womanliness during infancy and toddlerhood. Fathers are important then, but mothers are primary. At about three to five years of age, however, a lad gradually pulls away from his mom and sisters in an effort to formulate a masculine identity.[2] It is typical for boys during those years, and even earlier, to crave the attention and involvement of their dads and to try to emulate his behavior and mannerisms.

I remember my son clearly identifying with my masculinity when he was in that period between kindergarten and first grade. For example, as our family prepared to leave in the car, Ryan would say, "Hey, Dad. Us guys will get in the front seat and the girls will sit in the back." He wanted it known that he was a "guy" just like me. I was keenly aware that he was patterning his behavior and masculinity after mine. That's the way the system is supposed to work.

> "HEY, DAD. US GUYS WILL GET IN THE FRONT SEAT AND THE GIRLS WILL SIT IN THE BACK."

I was blessed to have a wonderful father who was accessible to me from the earliest years of childhood. I'm told that when I was two years of age, my family lived in a one-bedroom apartment, and my little bed was located beside that of my parents. My father said later that it was very common during that time for him to awaken at night to a little voice that was whis-

pering, "Daddy? Daddy?" My father would answer quietly, "What, Jimmy?" And I would say, "Hold my hand!" Dad would reach across the darkness and grope for my little hand, finally just engulfing it in his own. He said the instant he had my hand firmly in his grip, my arm would become limp and my breathing deep and regular. I'd immediately gone back to sleep. You see, I only wanted to know that he was there!

LEARNING RESPECT

Developing respect for parents is the critical factor in child management. It is imperative that a child learns to respect his parents—not to satisfy their egos, but because his relationship with them provides the basis for his later attitude toward all other people. Respect for parents must be maintained for another equally important reason. If you want your child to accept your values when he reaches his teen years, then you must be worthy of his respect during his younger days. When a child can successfully defy his parents during his first fifteen years, laughing in their faces and stubbornly flouting their authority, he develops a natural contempt for them. Viewing his parents as being unworthy of his respect, he may very well reject every vestige of their philosophy and faith.

This factor is also of vital importance to Christian parents who wish to transmit their love for Jesus Christ to their sons. Why? Because young children typically identify their parents . . . and especially their fathers . . . with God. Therefore, if Mom and Dad are not worthy of respect, then neither are their morals, their country, their values and beliefs, or even their religious faith.

I was shocked to see this close identification between God and me in the mind of my son when he was two years old. Ryan had watched his mother and me pray before we ate each meal, but he had never been asked to say grace. One day when I was out of town on a business trip, Shirley spontaneously turned to the toddler and asked if he would like to pray before they ate. The invitation startled him, but he folded his little hands, bowed his head, and said, "I love you, Daddy. Amen."

When I returned home and Shirley told me what had happened, the story unsettled me. I hadn't realized the degree to which Ryan linked me with his "heavenly Father." I wasn't even sure I wanted to stand in those shoes. It was too big a job, and I didn't want the responsibility. But I had no choice, nor do you. God has given us the assignment of representing Him during the formative years of parenting. That's why it is so critically important for us to acquaint our kids with God's two predominant natures. . . . His unfathomable love and His justice. If we love our children but permit them to treat us disrespectfully and with disdain, we have distorted their understanding of the Father. On the other hand, if we are rigid disciplinarians who show no love, we have tipped the scales in the other direction. What we teach our children about the Lord is a function, to some degree, of how we model love and discipline in our relationship with them.[1]

[1]Dr. James Dobson, *The New Dare to Discipline* (Wheaton, Ill.: Tyndale House Publishers, 1970, 1992), 18–20.

I have a catalog of warm memories of my dad from the preschool years. One day when I was nearly three, I was at home with my mother and heard a knock on the front door.

"Go see who it is," she said with a little smile on her face.

I opened the door and there stood my dad. He took my hand and said, "Come with me. I want to show you something." He led me to the side of the house, where he had hidden a big blue tricycle. It was one of the wonderful moments of my life. On another day during that same year, I recall trotting beside my big dad (he was six foot four) and feeling very proud to be with him. I even recall how huge his hand felt as it held mine.

I also remember the delightful times I roughhoused with my father. Many moms fail to understand why that kind of foolishness is important, but it is. Just as wolf cubs and leopard kittens romp and fight with each other, boys of all ages love to rumble. When I was five years old, my dad and I used to horrify BOYS OF ALL AGES LOVE TO RUMBLE. my mother by having all-out kick fights. That's right! *Kick fights!* He weighed 180 pounds and I tipped the scales at about 50, but we went at each other like sumo wrestlers. He would entice me to kick his shins and then, inevitably, he would block my thrust with the bottom of his foot.

That made me go after him again with a vengeance. Then Dad would tap

me on the shin with his toe. Believe it or not, this was wonderful fun for

me. We would end up laughing hysterically, despite the bumps and bruises

on my legs. My mother would demand that we stop, having no clue about

why I loved this game. It was just a guy thing.

I had a conversation once with a man named Bill Houghton, who was president of a large construction firm. Through the years, he had hired and managed thousands of employees. I asked him, "When you are thinking of hiring an employee—especially a man—what do you look for?" His answer surprised me. He said, "I look primarily at the relationship between the man and his father. If he felt loved by his dad and respected his authority, he's likely to be a good employee." The relationship between a boy and his father sets the tone for so much of what is to come. Dad is *that* important at home.

If character training is a primary goal of parenting, and I believe it is, then the best way to instill it is through the demeanor and behavior of a father.

THE RELATIONSHIP BETWEEN A BOY AND HIS FATHER SETS THE TONE FOR SO MUCH OF WHAT IS TO COME.

Identification with him is a far more efficient teacher than lecturing, scolding, punishing, bribing, and cajoling. Boys watch their dads intently, noting every minor detail of behavior and values. It is probably true in your home, too. Your sons will imitate much of what you do. If you are honest, trustworthy, caring, loving, self-disciplined, and God-fearing, your boys will be influenced by those traits as they age. If you are deeply committed to Jesus Christ and live by biblical principles, your children will probably follow in your footsteps. So much depends on what they observe in you, for better or worse.

Someone said, "I'd rather see a sermon than hear one." There is truth to this statement. Children may not remember what you say, but they are usually impacted for life by what you do. Consider the task of teaching your boys to be honest, for example. Yes, you should teach what the Scripture says about truthfulness, but you should also look for opportunities to live according to that standard of righteousness. I'm reminded of something that happened several years ago in the state of Georgia, when the Bulldogs of Rockdale County High School overcame a big deficit to win the state basketball championship. Coach Cleveland Stroud couldn't have been more proud of his team. But then a few days later, while watching the game films of the play-offs, he noticed that there was an ineligible player on the court for forty-five seconds during one of the games. He called the Georgia High School Association and reported the violation, costing the school the title and the trophy. When asked about it at a press conference, Coach Stroud said, "Some people have said that we should have kept quiet about it. That it was just forty-five seconds, and that the player wasn't really an impact player. But you gotta do what's honest and right. I told my team that people forget the scores of basketball games. They don't ever forget what you're made out of."[3]

"PEOPLE FORGET THE SCORES OF BASKETBALL GAMES. THEY DON'T EVER FORGET WHAT YOU'RE MADE OUT OF."

You can be certain that every member of the Bulldogs' team will remember the character of Coach Stroud. A letter to the editor of the local newspaper summed it up well. "We have scandals in Washington and cheating on Wall Street. Thank goodness we live in Rockdale County, where honor and integrity are alive and being practiced."[4]

Your boys and girls need to see you doing what is right, even when it is inconvenient to do so.

This raises a question about the other characteristics you are trying to model for your sons. Have you thought that through? Do you know exactly what you're trying to accomplish at home? Such a plan should begin, I

believe, with a personal commitment to Jesus Christ, who will guide your steps in the days ahead. It is not inappropriate for a man to feel things deeply or to reveal his inner passions and thoughts. Nor must he present a frozen exterior to the world around him. But at the same time, there is a definite place in manhood for strength and confidence in the midst of a storm, and that role falls more naturally to men. As a huge oak tree provides shelter and protection for all the living things that nest in its branches, a strong man provides security and comfort for every member of his family. He knows who he is as a child of God and what is best for his wife and children. His sons need such a man to look up to and to emulate. Men were designed to take care of the people they love, even if it involves personal sacrifice. When they fulfill that responsibility, their wives, sons, and daughters usually live in greater peace and harmony.

During the 1969 Christmas season, my father's two surviving brothers and his sister gathered in California for a family reunion. And on that happy occasion, they spent the better part of five days reminiscing

MEN WERE DESIGNED TO TAKE CARE OF THE PEOPLE THEY LOVE, EVEN IF IT INVOLVES PERSONAL SACRIFICE.

about their childhood and early home life. While all the conversations were of interest to me, there was a common thread that was especially significant throughout the week. It focused on the respect with which these four surviving siblings addressed the memories of their father (my grandfather). He died in 1935, a year before my birth, yet they spoke of him with unmistakable awe thirty-four years later. He still lived in their minds as a man of enormous character and strength. I asked them to explain the qualities that they admired so greatly but received little more than vague generalities.

"He was a tower of strength," said one.

"He had a certain dignity about him," said another, with appropriate gestures.

"We held him in awe," replied the third.

It is difficult to summarize the subtleties and complexities of the human personality, and they were unable to find the right words. Only when we began talking about specific remembrances did the personality of this patriarch become apparent. R. L. Dobson was one of the oak trees I mentioned—a man of strength and integrity.

HE LIVED BY AN INTERNAL STANDARD THAT WAS SINGULARLY UNCOMPROMISING.

Although not a Christian until shortly before his death, he lived by an internal standard that was singularly uncompromising. As a young man, for example, he invested heavily in a business venture with a partner whom he later discovered to be dishonest. When he learned of the chicanery, he walked out and virtually gave the company to the other man. That former partner built the corporation into one of the most successful operations in the South and became a multimillionaire. But my grandfather never looked back. He took a clean conscience with him to his grave.

There were other admirable traits, of course, and many of them were transmitted to my dad. These two men personified much of what I'm trying to convey in this examination of manhood. Then they passed those values down to me.

I urge those of you who are young fathers to provide that modeling on which your boys can build their masculine identities. As you carry out the traditional roles we have described, or some version of them, your sons will observe who you are and thereby learn to serve in a similar way when they are grown. That's why any advice to dads about raising boys must begin with an examination of their individual demeanor and character.

While modeling is the first way a father influences his son, the second way deals with specific instruction about day-to-day living that dads should transmit to their sons. This includes information passed on about everything from how a man should treat a woman to the best place to catch a walleye.

Begin these and other conversations early, geared to the age and maturity of the child. They must be well planned and carried out as the years unfold. Haven't you heard grown men say with conviction, "My father always told me . . ."? This is because the things emphasized during childhood often stay with a person throughout life, even if they haven't appeared to "stick" at the time. In short, this kind of specific instruction is the substance of your responsibility to affirm, recognize, and celebrate your son's journey into manhood.

I know the suggestions and ideas I have offered in this chapter put great pressure on us to be superdads, but that's just the way it is. I felt it too when our kids were small. Frankly, raising kids was a scary responsibility for Shirley and me. We knew we were inadequate to handle the job and that no one is capable of guaranteeing the outcome of that task. That's why we began praying diligently for the spiritual welfare of our children. Thousands of times through the years, we found ourselves on our knees asking for wisdom and guidance.

FRANKLY, RAISING KIDS WAS A SCARY RESPONSIBILITY.

Then we did the very best we could at home. Somehow, that seems to have been enough. Both of our children love the Lord today and are wonderful human beings. Shirley deserves most of the credit for the outcome, but I gave it my best effort too. Fortunately, parents do not have to be perfect in order to transmit their values to the next generation.

Our heavenly Father will also answer your prayers for your kids if you turn to Him.

Mothers and Sons

OKAY, MOM. Let's talk about what it means to be a boy and how you might relate better to them. Many women admit that raising boys has been a special challenge. They remember what it was like to be a frilly little girl, but they have only a vague notion of how their sons feel, think, and behave. Boys are bent on making messes, teasing the other siblings, racing through the house, and challenging every decision and order that comes their way.

One of my colleagues, Dr. Tim Irwin, shared his observation that women who have not grown up with brothers are often shocked by the sheer physicality of boys—by the sights and sounds and smells they generate. Some admit they are completely "clueless" in knowing how to deal with them. One obvious suggestion is to help boys release their excess energy by getting them involved in activities where fighting, laughing, running, tumbling, and yelling are acceptable. Soccer, karate, Little League, and football are a few possibilities. Moms also need to keep boys' little minds and hands busy. It's in their best interest to do so. My father once said about our energetic toddler, "If you let that kid get bored, you deserve what he's going to do to you." Shirley's stepfather, who has a South Dakota accent, once said after baby-sitting our kids for a week, "Oh, der good kids. You just gotta keep 'em out in da open." Good advice!

There's another characteristic of boys that I'll bet you've noticed. They ain't listening most of the time. They have a remarkable ability to ignore anything that doesn't interest them. Men are like that too. My wife can't understand how I am able to write a book, including this one, while a televised football game is blaring in the study. I don't actually watch and compose at the same time, but I can turn off the sound in my mind until I choose to hear it, such as when a replay appears on the screen. After watching for a moment, I go back to what I was doing.

THEY HAVE A REMARKABLE ABILITY TO IGNORE ANYTHING THAT DOESN'T INTEREST THEM.

Alas, boys have that same ability to ignore their moms. They honestly don't hear the words that are being poured into their ears. That is why I recommend that you as a mom reach out physically and touch your boys if you want to get their attention. When they turn to look at you, give them your message in short bursts.

A good relationship with your son begins when he is only a baby. There is no way to overstate the importance of what is called "infant bonding" between mother and child of either sex. The quality of early relationships between boys and their mothers is a powerful predictor of lifelong psychological and physical health.[5]

Children were designed to link emotionally with a mother and a father and to develop securely within the protection of their arms.

When our firstborn was two years old, I was finishing my doctoral work at the University of Southern California. Every available dollar was needed to support my tuition and related expenses. Although we didn't want Shirley to work when Danae was young, we felt we had no alternative. Shirley taught school and our little girl was taken to a day-care center each morning. One day when we arrived at the facility, Danae began to cry uncontrollably. "No! No! No, Daddy!" she said to me. She clung to my neck as I car- "No! No! No! Daddy!" ried her to the door and then begged me not to leave. Children at that age typically do not like to be left by parents, but this was something different. Danae had a look of terror in her eyes, and I suspected that she had been very upset the last time she was there. I could only imagine what had happened. I turned and walked back to the car carrying my precious daughter. When we were alone, I said, "Danae, I promise that you will never have to stay there again." And she never did.

Shirley and I talked about how we were going to keep my promise. We finally decided to sell and "eat" one of our two Volkswagens, which allowed her to stay home and take care of our daughter for a year. By the time the money was gone, I was out of school and we could afford for Shirley to be a full-time mom. Not everyone could do what we did, and certainly, there are millions of single parents out there who have no alternatives. If that is the case, you simply have to make the best of it. If a relative or a friend can keep your child during the day, that is better than a child-care facility, all things being equal. What is needed is continuity in the relationship between a child and the one who provides daily care.

The bottom line from many studies of infancy and early child development is consistent: babies have several essential emotional needs. Among them are touch, connection, permanence, nurturance, and reassurance. Sometimes I wish babies were born with a sign around their necks that warns, "Caution! Handle with Care! Love me. Protect me! Give me a place in your heart."

Despite the importance of an early mother-child bond, it may seem strange that little boys begin to pull away from their moms very early on. Boys, even more than girls, become negative at that time and resist any efforts to

THEY SAY NO TO EVERYTHING, EVEN TO THINGS THEY LIKE.

corral or manage them. They say no to everything, even to things they like. They run when called and scream bloody murder at bedtime. They usually respond better to fathers—but not very much. Believe it or not, this is a moment of opportunity for Mom. She *must* take charge during these delightful but challenging days of toddlerhood. It is not sufficient to leave the discipline solely to Dad. Respect for her authority and leadership are rooted in this period. Just remember that boys desperately need to be supervised. They also need to be "civilized," quite literally. In the absence of firm but loving leadership, they tend to follow their own selfish and destructive inclinations, which can be harmful to a boy and to other members of the family. What are the other implications for mothers during this period of disconnection and differentiation? For one thing, they should not allow themselves to feel rejected and wounded by their boys' gravitation toward fathers. Just remember that the behavior isn't personal. Boys are genetically programmed to respond that way. I remember feeling somewhat embarrassed by my mother's hugs and kisses when I was three years old. I told her one day that I thought it was "silly." Her wise response was, "I do too." I wanted and needed her love, but I was already aware of a strange

tug toward my dad. Although most kids won't be able to articulate that urge, what is happening is a healthy process from which manhood will flower in time. Mothers should encourage their husbands to be there for their sons when the need is the greatest. Show them this section of my book, even if they won't read the rest of it. Men tend to be extremely busy during the early years of parenthood, and their minds are on other things. A gentle nudge will get their attention better than inundating them with bucket loads of guilt and criticism.

Age ten for most boys is a lovable time. Some have called it an "angelic" period, when cooperation and obedience are at their peak. It will never be quite that way again. By eleven, the typical boy will probably be getting

testy and cantankerous. He may irritate his mother, tease his younger

brothers and sisters, and push the limits a little farther. That means testos-

terone is starting to flow and the adolescent upheaval is getting under way.

Then come twelve and thirteen. For the next three years, it's "Hang on to

your hat!"

My father and mother were faced with a difficult choice when I was sixteen

years old. Dad was an evangelist who was gone most of the time, while my

MY PARENTS GAVE PRIORITY   mother was home with me.
TO ME WHEN I WAS SLIDING
                               During the adolescent years, I
     CLOSE TO THE BRINK.   began to get testy with my mother.

I never went into total rebellion, but I was definitely flirting with the possi-

bility. I'll never forget the night my mom called my dad on the phone. I

was listening as she said, "I need you." To my surprise, my dad immediate-

ly cancelled a four-year slate of meetings, sold our home, and moved seven

hundred miles south to take a pastorate so he could be with me until I fin-

ished high school. It was an enormous sacrifice for him to make. He never

fully recovered professionally from it. But he and Mom felt my welfare was

more important than their immediate responsibilities. Dad was home with

me during those two volatile years when I could have gotten into serious

trouble. When I speak with reverence about my parents today, as I often

do, one of the reasons is because they gave priority to me when I was sliding close to the brink. Would you do the same for your teenagers?

You may not be called upon to make such a radical change in your lifestyle. Sometimes the solution is much simpler, such as making it a point to sit down and eat dinner together as often as possible.

"GIVE ME PUBERTY!"

The period of early adolescence is typically a painful time of life, marked by rapid physical and emotional changes. This characteristic difficulty was expressed by a seventh-grade boy who had been asked to recite Patrick Henry's historic speech at a special program commemorating the birth of the United States. But when the young man stood nervously before an audience of parents, he became confused and blurted out: "Give me puberty or give me death!" His statement is not as ridiculous as it sounds. Many teens sincerely believe they must choose between these dubious alternatives.

It is during this time that self-doubt and feelings of inferiority reach an all-time high, amidst the greatest social pressures yet experienced. Thus, relatively minor evidences of rejection or ridicule are of major significance to those who already see themselves as fools and failures. It is difficult to overestimate the impact of having no one to sit with on the school-sponsored bus trip, or of not being invited to an important event, or of being laughed at by the "in" group, or of waking up in the morning to find seven shiny new pimples on your bumpy forehead, or of being humiliated by the girl you thought had liked you as much as you liked her. Some boys consistently face this kind of social catastrophe throughout their teen years. They will never forget the experience.

We simply must remain in touch during these turbulent years. This is especially true for the formerly pleasant and happy child who seemingly degenerates overnight into a sour and critical fourteen-year-old anarchist. Not only are parents distressed by this radical change, but the child is often worried about it too. He may be confused by the resentment and hostility that have become so much a part of his personality. He clearly needs the patient reassurance of a loving parent who can explain the "normality" of this agitation and help him ventilate the accumulated tension. The task of prying open the door of communication with an angry adolescent can require more tact and skill than any other assignment in parenthood.

One of the most common mistakes of parenthood is to be drawn into verbal battles with our children, which leave us exhausted but without strategic advantage. Let me say it again: Don't yield to this impulse. Don't argue with your teen. Don't subject him to perpetual threats and finger-wagging accusations and insulting indictments. And most important, don't nag him endlessly.[1]

[1] Dr. James Dobson, *The Strong-Willed Child* (Wheaton, Ill.: Tyndale House Publishers, 1987), 190–191, 196–197, 202.

Parental involvement is the key to getting kids through the storms of adolescence. Family relationships are what matters to adolescents, and mealtimes can be a great time to relate. When parents have time for their kids, when they get together almost every day for conversation and interaction—in this case, while eating—their teens do much better in school and in life. Bottom line? Families bring stability and mental health to children and teens.

FAMILIES BRING STABILITY AND MENTAL HEALTH TO CHILDREN AND TEENS.

With determination and planning, we should be able to intersect each others' worlds at least once every day or two. The most important ingredient is not what's on the table—we can serve a home-cooked meal or call for a pasta delivery. What *does* make a difference is that we regularly set aside time to sit down and talk together.

Eating can also provide the centerpiece for family traditions, which give identity and belonging to each member. To cite our own circumstances again, we have designated foods for every holiday. It's turkey at Thanksgiving and Christmas, it's red beans and ham on New Year's Day, it's baked ham on Easter, it's barbecued hamburgers (made of turkey) on the Fourth of July, and it's Chinese food on Christmas Eve (don't ask me why). There are many dimensions to the various traditions, which go far beyond

the choice of foods. Each of us looks forward to those occasions, which are always filled with laughter, spontaneity, and meaning. Children love these kinds of recurring activities that bond them to their parents. I hope you have similar traditions of your own.

Finally, family mealtimes continue to be great settings in which to impart the truths of our faith. As the blessings of the day are recounted, children

see evidence of God's loving, faithful care and the importance of honoring

Him with a time

of thanks. In our

family, we never

AS THE BLESSINGS OF THE DAY ARE RECOUNTED, CHILDREN SEE EVIDENCE OF GOD'S LOVING, FAITHFUL CARE.

eat a meal without pausing first to express gratitude to the One who pro-

vides us with "every good and perfect gift" (James 1:17). I believe children

of Christian parents should be taught to "say grace" every time meals are

partaken. Parents can also use that talking time to discuss biblical principles

at the table and apply them to personal circumstances. Jesus used the time

of fellowship created around meals to present many of His teachings. Acts

2:46-47 gives us a glimpse of how significant sharing a meal was to the

early church by describing how believers "broke bread in their homes and

ate together with glad and sincere hearts, praising God."

The more your boys feel part of something loving and fun, the less they

will need to rebel against it. That's not a promise, just a probability.

Single Parents and Grandparents

TO EVERY SINGLE MOM who is striving to raise a son on her own, let me emphasize first that you have an invaluable resource in our heavenly Father. He created your children and they are precious to Him. How do I know that? Because He said repeatedly in His Word that He has a special tenderness for fatherless children and their mothers. There are many references in Scripture to their plight. For example:

- Deuteronomy 10:17-18: The Lord your God . . . defends the cause of the fatherless and the widow, and loves the alien, giving him food and clothing.

- Deuteronomy 27:19: Cursed is the man who withholds justice from the alien, the fatherless or the widow.

- Psalm 68:5: A father to the fatherless, a defender of widows, is God in his holy dwelling.

- Zechariah 7:10: Do not oppress the widow or the fatherless, the alien or the poor.

The message is very clear, isn't it? The Lord is watching over the oppressed, the poor, the downtrodden, and the child who has no father. And yes, He is concerned about your children too. He is waiting for you to ask Him for help. I have seen miraculous answers to prayer on behalf of those who have sought His help in what seemed like impossible situations.

My own wife, Shirley, was a product of a broken home. Her father was an alcoholic who abused the family and squandered their meager resources in a local bar. Soon, the marriage ended in divorce. At that critical moment, Shirley's mom recognized that she was going to need help raising her two kids alone, so she sent them to a little evangelical church in the neighborhood. There they met Jesus Christ and found the stability they lacked at home. Shirley began praying in the quietness of her little bedroom that the Lord would send a father to love and take care of them. He did precisely

that. Along came a wonderful thirty-seven-year-old man named Joe who had never been married. He became a Christian and a marvelous father to the two kids. Joe gave them stability through the rest of childhood and adolescence. He has been my father-in-law now for forty years, and I love him like my own dad. So you see, even though the probabilities and predictions are that remarriage is risky, anything is possible when you depend on God and look to Him for strength. I will leave it to you and your pastor

RECRUIT A GOOD MENTOR

In her book *Mothers and Sons,* the late Jean Lush talked about the challenges single mothers face in raising sons. She says that ages four to six are especially important and difficult.[1]

I agree. If he has a father in the home, he'll usually want to spend more time with his dad apart from his mother and sisters. If his dad is not accessible to him, a substitute must be found.

Admittedly, good mentors can be difficult to recruit. Consider your friends, relatives, or neighbors who can offer as little as an hour or two a month. In a pinch, a mature high schooler who likes kids could even be "rented" to play ball or go fishing with a boy in need.

If you belong to a church, you should be able to find support for your son among the male members of the Christian community. Scripture commands people of faith to care for children without fathers. Isaiah 1:17 states, "Defend the cause of the fatherless, plead the case of the widow." Jesus Himself took boys and girls on His lap and said, "And whoever welcomes a little child like this in my name welcomes me" (Matthew 18:5). I believe it is our responsibility as Christian men to help single mothers with their difficult parenting tasks.

Certainly single mothers have many demands on their time and energy, but the effort to find a mentor for their sons might be the most worthwhile contribution they can make.[2]

[1] Jean Lush, "Mothers and Sons," *Focus on the Family,* 5–6 March 1991.

[2] Dr. James Dobson, *Complete Marriage and Family Home Reference Guide* (Wheaton, Ill.: Tyndale House Publishers, 2000), 207–208.

to determine whether or not you have biblical grounds to remarry, which can be another thorny issue to be determined.

Until a good man like Joe comes along, you as a single mother must make an all-out effort to find a father-substitute for your boys. An uncle or a neighbor or a coach or a musical director or a Sunday-school teacher may do the trick. Placing your boys under the influence of such a man for even a single hour per week can make a great difference. Get them involved in Boy Scouts, Boy's Club, soccer, or Little League. Give your boys biographies, and take them to movies or rent videos that focus on strong masculine (but moral) heroes. However you choose to solve the problem, do not let the years go by without a man's influence in the lives of your boys. If they have no nurturing male role models by which to pattern themselves, they will turn to whoever is available, such as gang members, or perhaps to you, the mom. But it is not healthy for boys to model themselves exclusively after their mothers.

You should train and guide your children in the same ways you would if your marriage was intact. They need boundaries even more than the children of intact families. An authoritative but loving mother brings security to a child for whom everything seems insecure. Get in there and lead! Punish when punishment is needed. Hug them when they need reassurance. And make them think you know what you're doing and where you're going even when you may not have a clue.

IF YOU ARE A DEDICATED MOM WHO GIVES PRIORITY TO YOUR CHILDREN, THEY WILL DO ALL RIGHT.

Now let me offer some additional hope and advice to single mothers. If you are a dedicated mom who gives priority to your children, they will do all right.

Grandparents

Let me turn now to the people who are most likely to give you the help you need. I'm referring to maternal or paternal grandparents. They have a

God-given responsibility to influence their grandkids, and most of them are more than willing to fit the bill. Our organization just published a helpful book that may stimulate some ideas. It is called *The Gift of Grandparenting,* by Eric Wiggen. Here are some excerpts from it that will, I hope, not only motivate single parents to look to their parents but will also inspire grandparents to get more involved with their grandkids. These are the considered words of Eric Wiggen:

Young people who visit their grandparents, with few exceptions, do so because they want—often very badly—the companionship of their elders. The same grandmother who beat me at checkers when I was nine became a friend in whom I could confide when I was nineteen. She wrote me letters, long and full of family news. When I came home from college, we talked. And you know what? Grandma wanted to listen to me! I soon found that she was fascinated with what I had to say, and she had more time to listen to me than my parents had. For your teen or single young-adult grandchildren, perhaps the most important "entertainment" you can give them is to listen when they talk.[6]

> "THE SAME GRANDMOTHER WHO BEAT ME AT CHECKERS . . . BECAME A FRIEND IN WHOM I COULD CONFIDE."

A sage once remarked that the elderly slow down and stoop over so that they can see things as children once again, so that they can hold the hands of children who toddle along on inexperienced feet. That bug on the sidewalk, the snail under the cabbage leaf, the robin pulling the worm from the rain-moistened earth—these are the things small children and their grandparents notice.[7]

Our grandchildren live in imperfect homes, reared by imperfect parents: our sons and daughters who are married to our sons-in-law or daughters-in-law, all of them imperfect. Although we all made mistakes raising our children, the good news is that as godly grandparents, walking with the Lord, we can expect the Lord to use us. Because of our own immaturity when our children—now parents—were growing up, we may have disap-

pointed them. But by keeping us alive to enjoy our grandchildren, the Lord is giving us a ministry to help fill in these gaps in our imperfect child-rearing.[8]

We grandparents must first firmly retake the lead, if not of society as a whole, at least of our own families. This is not as drastic a step as it may seem, for the pendulum has begun to swing the other way, and maturity is coming into fashion again.[9]

As grandparents, we desire to help usher our Brandons and Meghans across the threshold of adulthood. We can best do this when we realize that these youth, who much of the time are carefree and happy, are also suffering *through the most trying years of life—from puberty to young maturity. We gently criticize their behavior when we must. We set guidelines and expectations when they're entrusted to our care. Even as we wouldn't question another adult's toupée or hairdo, we avoid personal remarks about our emerging adult-teens whose souls may have been torn and trampled already in the school gauntlet or by conflicts at home. But most of all, we support, we listen, we pray. And we love.*[10]

I can't conclude this discussion without speaking directly, and perhaps boldly, to Christians who live in intact families. You have been reading in this chapter about the challenges faced by single parents. I hope you will consider the ways you might help. Men, how about taking the sons of single mothers with your own boys when you're going fishing or out to a ball game? Let those fatherless boys know that you care for them. Answer their questions and teach them how to throw a ball or how to block and tackle. This is not simply my own casual suggestion. It is a divine commandment. Remember the Scriptures I shared about God's compassion for fatherless children? Jesus conveyed that same love to the young. He took boys and girls on His lap and said, "Whoever welcomes a little child . . . in my name welcomes me" (Matthew 18:5).

To married moms, I hope you will reach out to the single mother and help

"WHOEVER WELCOMES A LITTLE CHILD . . . IN MY NAME WELCOMES ME." (MATTHEW 18:5)

her cope with the child-rearing task. Baby-sit for her so she can get out every now and then. Share your financial resources with those who have less, and include them in your holiday activities. You might be able to keep a single mom from going over the edge by giving her just a little encouragement and assistance. The Lord will reward you, I believe, for caring for someone who is desperate for a friend.

With that, we will close our discussion of single parents and grandparents with two more simple thoughts. The first concerns the difficult task of letting go when the job is done. That can be a very emotional time, especially for a mom who has labored, sweated, prayed, cried, scrimped, saved, cooked, cleaned, taught, and shepherded her children through numerous crises without the help of a husband or a father for her kids. All of a sudden, at the other end of childhood, the reason for her existence and her passion in living has to be surrendered. Her children have grown up. The empty place inside as her sons and daughters leave home can be like a chasm. After all these years, she is alone again.

My office at Focus on the Family sits across the valley from the United States Air Force Academy. From there I can see the cadets as they train to be pilots and officers. I particularly enjoy watching the gliders soaring through the heavens. The only way those graceful yellow crafts can fly is to be tethered to a powered plane that takes them up to where they can catch a wind current. Then they disengage and sail free and alone until returning to land.

While watching that beautiful spectacle one day, I recognized an analogy between flying and child rearing as a single parent. There is a time when your children need to be towed by the "mother plane." If that assistance were not available, or if it were not accepted, the "glider" would never get off the ground. But, inevitably, there comes an appropriate moment for a young pilot to disengage and soar free and alone in the blue heavens. Both operations are neces-

THERE IS A TIME WHEN YOUR CHILDREN NEED TO BE TOWED BY THE "MOTHER PLANE."

sary for successful flight. If you as a parent are not there for your kids when they are young, they are likely to remain "grounded" for life. On the other hand, if they stay tethered to you as young adults, they will never experience the thrill of independent flight. Letting go not only gives freedom to your grown son or daughter but allows you to soar as well. It's all part of the divine plan.

Some Assembly Required

RAISING HEALTHY, well-educated, self-disciplined children who love God and their fellow human beings is, I believe, the most challenging responsibility in living. Not even rocket science can approach it for complexity and unpredictability. And of course, the job is even more difficult today when the culture undermines and contradicts everything Christian parents are trying to accomplish at home.

Fortunately, we are not asked to do everything perfectly as moms and dads. Our kids usually manage to survive our mistakes and failures and turn out better than we have any right to boast about. I certainly made my share of mistakes as a father. Like millions of other men of my era, I often had a tough time balancing the pressure of my profession with the needs of my family. Not that I ever became an "absentee father," but I did struggle at times to be as accessible as I should have been. As it happened, my first book, *Dare to Discipline,* was published the same week that our second

SPEAKING A KIND WORD

Most children and adults are keenly interested in what their associates think and say. As a result, verbal reinforcement can be the strongest motivator of human behavior. Consider the tremendous impact of the following comments:

"Here comes Phil—the ugliest guy in school."

"Joe will strike out. He always does."

These unkind words burn like acid to the children they describe, causing them to modify future behavior. Phil may become quiet, withdrawn, and easily embarrassed. Joe may give up baseball and other athletic endeavors.

It happened to me, in fact. I have always thought of myself as a "jock," playing various sports through the years. I lettered in college tennis all four years and captained the team when I was a senior. However, I never had much interest in baseball . . . and for good reason. When I was in the third grade, I stood in right field one day with the bases loaded. The entire third grade class . . . including many girls . . . had turned out to watch the big game, and everything was on the line. The batter slugged a routine fly ball in my direction, which inexplicably went through my fingers and straight to the ground. I picked up the ball in my embarrassment and threw it to the umpire. He stepped aside and let it roll for fifty yards. I can still hear the runner's feet pounding toward home plate. I can still hear the girls laughing. I can still feel my hot face out there in right field. I walked off the field that day and gave up a brilliant baseball career.

Verbal reinforcement should permeate the entire parent-child relationship. Too often our parental instruction consists of a million "don'ts," which are jammed down the child's throat. We should spend more time rewarding him for the behavior we desire, even if our "reward" is nothing more than a sincere compliment. Remembering the child's need for self-esteem and acceptance, the wise parent can satisfy those important longings while using them to teach valued concepts and behavior. A couple examples may be helpful:

Father to son: "I appreciate your being quiet while I was figuring the income tax, Son. You were very thoughtful. Now that I have that job done, I'll have more time. Why don't we plan to go to the zoo next Saturday?"

Mother to husband in son's presence: "Neil, did you notice how Dan put his bicycle in the garage tonight? He used to leave it out until we told him to put it away; he is becoming much more responsible, don't you think?"[1]

[1]Dr. James Dobson, *The New Dare to Discipline* (Wheaton, Ill.: Tyndale House Publishers, 1970, 1992), 92–94.

child, Ryan, arrived. A baby always turns a house upside down, but the reaction to my book added to the turmoil. I was a full-time professor at a medical school, and yet I was inundated by thousands of letters and requests of every sort. There was no mechanism to handle this sudden notoriety. I remember flying to New York one Thursday night, doing seventeen television shows and press interviews in three days, and returning to work on Monday morning. It was nothing short of overwhelming.

My father, who always served as a beacon in dark times, saw what was happening to me and wrote a letter that was to change my life. First he congratulated me on my success, but then he warned that all the success in the world would not compensate if I failed at home. He reminded me that the spiritual welfare of our children was my most important responsibility and that the only way to build their faith was to model it personally and then to stay on my knees in prayer. That couldn't be done if I invested every resource in my profession. I have never forgotten that profound advice.

It eventually led to my resignation from the university and to the development of a ministry that permitted me to stay at home. I quit accepting speaking requests, started a radio program that required no travel, and refused to do "book tours" or accept other lengthy responsibilities that would take me away from my family. As I look back on that era today, I am so grateful that I chose to preserve my relationship with my children. The closeness that we enjoy today can be traced to that decision to make time for them when they needed me most. I could easily have made the greatest mistake of my life at that time.

AS I LOOK BACK ON THAT ERA TODAY, I AM SO GRATEFUL THAT I CHOSE TO PRESERVE MY RELATIONSHIP WITH MY CHILDREN.

I'm sure many fathers will read this response and find themselves today where I was back then. If you are one of them, I urge you to give priority to your family. Those kids around your feet will be grown and gone before you know it. Don't let the opportunity of these days slip away from you. No professional accomplishment or success is worth that cost. When you stand where I am today, the relationship with those you love will outweigh every other good thing in your life.

Yes, it has never been easy to raise healthy and productive children. After all, babies come into the world with no instructions, and you pretty much have to assemble them on your own. They are also maddeningly complex, and there are no guaranteed formulas that work in every instance. And finally, the techniques that succeed magnificently with one child can fail bewilderingly with another.

LOVING LEADERSHIP

Parental power can be defined as a hostile form of manipulation in order to satisfy adult purposes. As such it disregards the best interests of the child on whom it tramples and produces a relationship of fear and intimidation. Drill instructors in the Marine Corps have been known to depend on this form of power to indoctrinate their beleaguered recruits.

Proper authority, by contrast, is defined as loving leadership. Without decision makers and others who agree to follow, there is inevitable chaos and confusion and disorder in human relationships. Loving authority is the glue that holds social orders together, and it is absolutely necessary for the healthy functioning of a family.

There were times when I said to my son, "Ryan, you are tired because you were up too late last night. I want you to brush your teeth right now and put on your pajamas." My words may sound like a suggestion, but Ryan would be wise to remember who's making it. I do not always have time to negotiate, nor do I feel obligated in every instance to struggle for compromises. I have the *authority* to do what I think is in Ryan's best interest, and there are times when I expect him not to negotiate, but to *obey*. His learning to yield to my loving leadership is excellent training for his later submission to the loving authority of God. This is very different from the use of vicious and hostile power, resulting from the fact that I outweigh him.[1]

[1] Dr. James Dobson, *The Strong-Willed Child* (Wheaton, Ill.: Tyndale House Publishers, 1987), 179–180.

PARENTING PRINCIPLES

Let me summarize my approach to child rearing by stating its opposite. I am not recommending that your home be harsh and oppressive. I am not suggesting that you give your children a spanking every morning with their ham and eggs or that you make your boys sit in the living room with their hands folded and their legs crossed. I am not proposing that you try to make adults out of your kids so you can impress your adult friends with your parental skill, or that you punish your children whimsically, swinging and screaming when they didn't know they were wrong. I am not suggesting that you insulate your dignity and authority by being cold and unapproachable. These parental tactics do not produce healthy, responsible children. By contrast, I am recommending a simple principle: When you are defiantly challenged, win decisively. When the child asks, "Who's in charge?" tell him. When he mutters, "Who loves me?" take him in your arms and surround him with affection. Treat him with respect and dignity, and expect the same in return. Then begin to enjoy the sweet benefits of competent parenthood.[1]

[1] Dr. James Dobson, *Complete Marriage and Family Home Reference Guide* (Wheaton, Ill.: Tyndale House Publishers, 2000), 107.

This difficulty in raising children is a recurring theme in the letters we receive at Focus on the Family. We have heard it so often, in fact, that we decided to conduct a poll to ascertain the common frustrations of parenting. The answers received from more than a thousand mothers and fathers were very revealing. Some responded with humor, especially those who were raising toddlers. They told the most delightful stories about sticky telephones, wet toilet seats, and knotted shoestrings. Their experiences reminded me of the days when Shirley and I were chasing ambitious preschoolers.

Tell me why it is that a toddler never throws up in the bathroom? Never! To do so would violate some great unwritten law of the universe. It is even more difficult to understand why he or she will gag violently at the sight of a perfectly wonderful breakfast of oatmeal, eggs, bacon, and orange juice— and then go play in the toilet. I have no idea what makes a kid do that. I only know that it drives a mother crazy!

Unfortunately, the majority of those who responded to our questionnaire did not share funny stories about cute kids. Many of them were experiencing considerable frustration in their parenting responsibilities. Rather than being critical of their children, however, most said they were troubled by their inadequacies as mothers and fathers!

Their answers, including these actual responses, revealed the self-doubt that is prevalent among parents today:

- I don't know how to cope with my children's problems.

- I'm not able to make the kids feel secure and loved.

- I've lost confidence in my ability to parent.

- I've failed my children.

- I'm not the example I should be.

- I see my own bad habits and character traits in my children.

- I'm unable to relate to my children.

- I feel guilty when it seems that I have failed my kids.

- I'm unable to cope.

- I know it's too late to go back and do it right.

- I'm overwhelmed by the responsibility of it all.

Isn't it incredible to observe just how tentative we have become about this task of raising children? Parenting is hardly a new technology. Since Adam and Eve graced the Garden, perhaps 15 billion people have lived on this earth, yet we've become increasingly nervous about bringing up the baby. It is a sign of the times.

Mothers, especially, have been blamed for everything that can conceivably go wrong with children. Even when their love and commitment are incalculable, the experts accuse them of making grievous errors in toilet training, disciplining, feeding, medicating, and educating their youngsters. They are either overpossessive or undernurturing. Their approach is either harsh or permissive. One psychiatrist even wrote an entire book on the dangers of religious training, blaming parents for scaring kids with talk of

MOTHERS . . . HAVE BEEN BLAMED FOR EVERYTHING THAT CAN CONCEIVABLY GO WRONG WITH CHILDREN.

the next world. Thus, no matter how diligently Mom approaches her parenting responsibilities, she is likely to be accused of twisting and warping her children.

Perhaps this explains why women are more critical of themselves than men are. Eighty percent of the respondents to our poll were women, and their most frequent comment was "I'm a failure as a mother!" What nonsense! Women have been taught to think of themselves in this way, and it is time to set the record straight.

The task of procreation was never intended to be so burdensome. Of course it is demanding. And children are challenging, to be sure. But the guilt and self-doubt that often encumber the parenting responsibility are not part of the divine plan. Throughout the Scriptures, the raising of children is presented as a wonderful blessing from God—a welcome, joyful experience. And today, it remains one of the greatest privileges in life to bring a baby into the world to love and care for. What a wonderful opportunity it is to teach these little ones to revere God with all their hearts and to serve others throughout their lives.

Promoting Peace

IF AMERICAN WOMEN were asked to indicate the most irritating feature of child rearing, I'm convinced that sibling rivalry would get their unanimous vote. Little children (and older ones too) are not content just to hate each other in private. They attack one another like miniature warriors, mobilizing their troops and probing for a weakness in the defensive line. They argue, hit, kick, scream, grab toys, taunt, tattle, and sabotage the opposing forces.

Sibling rivalry is difficult to "cure," but it can certainly be treated. It's not new, of course. It was responsible for the first murder on record (when Cain killed Abel) and has been represented in virtually every two-child family from that time to this. The underlying source of this conflict is old-fashioned jealousy and competition between children.

The first step is to avoid circumstances that compare children unfavorably with each other. The question is not "How am I doing?" It is "How am I doing compared with John or Steven or Marion?" The issue is not how fast can I run, but who crosses the finish line first. A boy does not care how tall he is; he is vitally interested in "who is tallest." Each child systematically measures himself against his peers and is tremendously sensitive to failure within his own family.

Accordingly, guard against comparative statements that routinely favor one child over another. This is particularly true in three areas. First, children are extremely sensitive about the matter of physical attractiveness and body characteristics. Anything that parents utter on this subject within the hearing of children should be screened carefully. It has the power to make brothers and sisters hate one another.

A BOY DOES NOT CARE HOW TALL HE IS; HE IS VITALLY INTERESTED IN "WHO IS TALLEST."

Second, the matter of intelligence is another sensitive nerve to be handled with care. It is not uncommon to hear parents say in front of their children, "I think the younger one is actually brighter than his brother." Adults find it difficult to comprehend how powerful that kind of assessment can be in a child's mind. Even when the comments are unplanned and spoken offhandedly, they convey how a child is seen within the family. We are all vulnerable to that bit of evidence.

WHO'S TOUGHEST?

Boys care about the issue of "who's toughest." Whenever a youngster moves into a new neighborhood or a new school district, he usually has to fight (either verbally or physically) to establish himself in the hierarchy of strength. Anyone who understands children knows that there is a "top dog" in every group, and there is a poor defeated little pup at the bottom of the heap. And every child between those extremes knows where he stands in relation to the others.

This respect for strength and courage also makes children want to know how "tough" their leaders are. They will occasionally disobey parental instructions for the precise purpose of testing the determination of those in charge. Thus whether you are a parent or grandparent, I can guarantee that sooner or later, one of the children under your authority will clench his little fist and challenge your leadership.

When a parent refuses to accept his child's defiant challenge, something changes in their relationship. The youngster begins to look at his mother or father with disrespect; that parent is unworthy of his allegiance. More important, he wonders why he or she would let him do such harmful things if he or she really loved him. The ultimate paradox of childhood is that kids want to be led by their parents, but they insist that their mothers and fathers earn the right to lead them.

It is obvious that children are aware of the contest of wills between generations, and that is precisely why the parental response is so important.

When a child behaves in ways that are disrespectful or harmful to himself or others, his hidden purpose is often to verify the stability of the boundaries. This testing has much the same function as a policeman who turns doorknobs at places of business after dark. Though he tries to open doors, he hopes they are locked and secure. Likewise, a child who assaults the loving authority of his parents is greatly reassured when their leadership holds firm and confident. He finds his greatest security in a structured environment where the rights of other people (and his own) are protected by definite boundaries.[1]

[1]Dr. James Dobson, *The Strong-Willed Child* (Wheaton, Ill.: Tyndale House Publishers, 1987), 15–16, 18, 30.

Third, children (especially boys) are extremely competitive with regard to athletic abilities. Those who are slower, weaker, and less coordinated than their brothers are rarely able to accept "second best" with grace and dignity.

Consider, for example, the following note given to me by the mother of two boys. It was written by a nine-year-old boy to his eight-year-old brother the evening after the younger child had beaten him in a race.

Dear Jim:

I am the greatest and your the badest. And I can beat everybody in a race and you can't beat anybody in a race. I'm the smartest and your the dumbest. I'm the best sport player and your the badest sport player. And your also a hog. I can beat anybody up. And that's the truth. And that's the end of this story.

> *Yours truly,*
> *Richard*

This note is humorous to me because Richard's motive was so poorly disguised. He had been badly stung by his humiliation on the field of honor, so he came home and raised the battle flags. He probably spent the next eight weeks looking for opportunities to fire torpedoes into Jim's soft underbelly. Such is the nature of mankind.

Am I suggesting, then, that parents eliminate all aspects of individuality within family life or that healthy competition should be discouraged? Definitely not. I am saying that in matters relative to good looks, brains, and athletic ability, each child should know that in his parents' eyes, he is respected and has equal worth with his siblings. Praise and criticism at home should be distributed as evenly as possible, although some children will inevitably be more successful in the outside world.

Sibling rivalry is also at its worst when there is no reasonable system of justice in the home—where the "lawbreakers" do not get caught or, if apprehended, are set free without standing trial. It is important to understand that laws in a society are established and enforced for the purpose of protecting people from each other. Individual families are similar to societies in their need for law and order. In the absence of justice, "neighboring" siblings begin to assault one another. The older child is bigger and tougher, which allows him to oppress his younger brothers and sisters. But the junior member of the family is not without weapons of his own. He strikes back by breaking the toys and prized possessions of the older sibling and interferes when friends are visiting. Mutual hatred then erupts like an angry volcano, spewing its destructive contents on everyone in its path.

HE STRIKES BACK BY BREAKING THE TOYS AND PRIZED POSSESSIONS OF THE OLDER SIBLING.

Nevertheless, when the children appeal to their parents for intervention, they are often left to fight it out among themselves. In many homes, the parents do not have sufficient disciplinary control to enforce their judgments. In others, they are so exasperated with constant bickering among siblings that they refuse to get involved. In still others, parents require an older child to live with an admitted injustice "because your sister is smaller than you." Thus, they tie his hands and render him utterly defenseless against the mischief of his bratty little brother or sister. Even more commonly today, mothers and fathers are both working while their children are at home busily disassembling each other.

I will say it again: One of your most important responsibilities is to establish an equitable system of justice and a balance of power at home. For purposes of illustration, let me list the boundaries and rules that evolved through the years when Danae and Ryan were at home:

- Neither child is *ever* allowed to make fun of the other in a destructive way. Period! This is an inflexible rule with no exceptions.
- Each child's room is his private territory. There are locks on both doors, and permission to enter is a revocable privilege. (Families with more than one child in each bedroom can allocate available living space for each youngster.)
- The older child is not permitted to tease the younger child.
- The younger child is forbidden to harass the older child.
- The children are not required to play with each other when they prefer to be alone or with other friends.
- We mediate any genuine conflict as quickly as possible, being careful to show impartiality and extreme fairness.

As with any plan of justice, this plan requires (1) respect for leadership of

the parent, (2) willingness by the parent to mediate, and (3) occasional enforcement or punishment. When this approach is accomplished with love, the emotional tone of the home can be changed from one of hatred to (at least) tolerance.

It would be naïve to miss the true meaning of sibling conflict: It often represents a form of manipulation of parents. Quarreling and fighting provide an opportunity for both children to "capture" adult attention. One father told me that his son and his nephew began to argue and then beat each other with their fists. Both fathers were nearby and decided to let the fight run its natural course. During the first lull in the action, one of the boys glanced sideways toward the passive men and said, "Isn't anybody going to stop us before we get hurt?!" The fight, you see, was something neither boy wanted. Their violent combat was directly related to the presence of the two adults and would have taken a different form if the boys had been alone. Children will often "hook" their parents' attention and intervention in this way.

"ISN'T ANYBODY GOING TO STOP US BEFORE WE GET HURT?!"

Believe it or not, this form of sibling rivalry is easiest to control. The parent must simply render the behavior unprofitable to each participant. I would recommend that a modified version of the following "speech" be given to quarreling children, depending on the age and circumstances: "Now listen carefully. If the two of you want to pick on each other and make yourselves miserable, then be my guests [assuming there is a fairly equal balance of power between them]. Go outside and argue until you're exhausted. But it's not going to occur under my feet anymore. It's over! And you know that I mean business when I make that kind of statement. Do we understand each other?"

Having made the boundaries clear, I would act decisively the *instant* either boy returned to his bickering in my presence. If they had separate bedrooms, I would confine one child to each room for at least thirty minutes of complete boredom—without radio, computer, or television. Or I would assign one to clean the garage and the other to mow the lawn. Or I would make them take a nap. My avowed purpose would be to make them believe me the next time I asked for peace and tranquillity.

It is simply not necessary to permit children to destroy the joy in living. And what is most surprising is that children are the happiest when their parents enforce reasonable limits with love and dignity.

Staying Close

P ARENTS TODAY MUST WORK harder
than ever at building satisfying and affirming relationships with
their kids. They must give kids a desire to stay within the confines
of the family and conform to its system of beliefs.

When I was a kid, parents didn't have to depend as much on communication and closeness to keep their children in line. They could control and
protect them, more or less, by the imposition of rules and the isolation of
their circumstances. Farmer John could take sassy little Johnny out to the
back forty acres and set his mind straight. Just the threat of that happening
was enough to keep most teens from going off the deep end.

My folks understood that system. They had a million rules. There were reg-
ulations and prohibitions for almost every imaginable situation. Coming
from a minister's home in a very conservative church, I was not allowed to

go to the movies (which were remarkably tame), or to dances, or even to use mild slang. I remember being reprimanded once for saying, "Hot Dog!" when I got excited about something. I'm still not sure what danger those words conveyed to my dad, but he warned me not to say them again. *Darn* was seen as a euphemism for *damn, geez* meant Jesus, *dad-gummit* (an old southern expression) was an obvious misrepresentation of God's name. I

I DARED NOT UTTER ANYTHING THAT EVEN VAGUELY RESEMBLED PROFANITY.

dared not utter anything that even vaguely resembled profanity, even if it was nonsensical. My cousin, who lived under the same general regime, invented a slang word called *gerrit* that he could use without being accused of saying something bad. "I'm sick of that gerrit school," he might say. The invention didn't work. *Gerrit* got banned too.

In those days, parental authority typically stood like a great shield against the evils in what was called "the world." Anything perceived as unwholesome or immoral was kept outside the white picket fence simply by willing it to stay put. Fortunately, the surrounding community was helpful to parents. It was organized to keep kids on the straight and narrow. Censorship kept the movies from going too far, schools maintained strict discipline, infractions were reported to the parents, truant officers prevented students from playing hooky, chaperones usually preserved virginity, alcohol was not

sold to minors, and illicit drugs were unheard-of. Even adults outside the family saw it as their civic responsibility to help protect children from anything that could harm them, whether physically, emotionally, or spiritually. Most of these townsfolk were probably acquainted with the children's parents, so it was easier for them to intervene. This support system didn't always do the job, of course, but it was generally effective.

Considering how the world has changed, it is doubly important to build relationships with boys from their earliest childhood. It still makes sense to prohibit harmful or immoral behavior, but those prohibitions must be supplemented by an emotional closeness that makes children want to do what is right. They must know that you love them unconditionally and that everything you require of them is for their own good. It is also helpful to explain why you want them to behave in certain ways. "Laying down the law" without this emotional linkage is likely to fail.

Author and speaker Josh McDowell expressed this principle in a single sentence. He said, "Rules without relationship lead to rebellion."[11] He is absolutely right. With all the temptations buzzing around our kids, simply saying no a thousand times creates a spirit of defiance.

SIMPLY SAYING NO A THOUSAND TIMES CREATES A SPIRIT OF DEFIANCE.

We have to build bridges to them from the ground up. The construction should begin early and include having fun as a family, laughing and joking, playing board games, throwing or kicking a ball, shooting baskets, playing Ping-Pong, running with the dog, talking at bedtime, and doing a thousand other things that tend to cement the generations together. The tricky part is to establish those friendships while maintaining parental authority and respect. It can be done. It must be done.

CAN'T BUY ME LOVE

Building relationships with children does not require large amounts of money. In fact, there are few conditions that inhibit a sense of appreciation more than for a child to feel he is entitled to whatever he wants, whenever he wants it. It is enlightening to watch as a boy tears open stacks of presents at a birthday party or perhaps at Christmastime. One after another, the expensive contents are tossed aside with little more than a glance. The child's mother is made uneasy by his lack of enthusiasm and appreciation, so she says, "Oh Marvin! Look what it is. It's a little tape recorder! What do you say to Grandmother? Give Grandmother a big hug. Did you hear me, Marvin? Go give Grams a big hug and kiss."

Marvin may or may not choose to make the proper noises to Grandmother. His lack of exuberance results from the fact that prizes that are won cheaply are of little value, regardless of the cost to the original purchaser. If you never allow a child to want something, he never enjoys the pleasure of receiving it. If you buy him a tricycle before he can walk, a bicycle before he can ride, a car before he can drive, and a diamond ring before he knows the value of money, he accepts these gifts with little pleasure and less appreciation. How unfortunate that such a child never had the chance to long for something, dreaming about it at night and plotting for it by day. He might have even gotten desperate enough to work for it. The same possession that brought a yawn could have been a trophy and a treasure. We parents, in our great love for our children, can do irreparable harm by yielding to their pleas for more and more things. There are times when the very best reply we can offer is . . . no.[1]

[1]Dr. James Dobson, *The New Dare to Discipline* (Wheaton, Ill.: Tyndale House Publishers, 1970, 1992), 44, 46, 48.

Building relationships with children does not require large amounts of money. A lifelong bond often emerges from traditions that give meaning to family time together. Let's describe what we mean by traditions. They refer to those repetitive activities that give identity and belonging to every member of the family. In the Broadway musical *Fiddler on the Roof,* remember that the fiddler was perched securely on top of the house because of tradition. Tradition told every member of the Jewish community who he or she was and how to deal with the demands of life and even what to wear. There is comfort and security for children when they know what is expected and how they fit into the scheme of things.

Children love daily routines and activities of the simplest kind. They want to hear the same story or the same joke until Mom and Dad are ready to climb the wall. And yet, these interactions are sometimes more appreciated by kids than are expensive toys or special events.

Beloved author and professor Dr. Howard Hendricks once asked his grown children what they remembered most fondly from their childhood. Was it the vacations they took or the trips to theme parks or the zoo? "No," they answered. It was when Dad got on the floor and wrestled with them. That's the way children think. It is especially the way boys think. A CLOSE-KNIT FAMILY IS WHAT KEEPS BOYS GROUNDED. The most meaningful activities in the family are often those simple interactions that build lasting connections between generations.

A close-knit family is what keeps boys grounded when the world is urging them to break loose. In this day, you dare not become disconnected during the time when everything is on the line.

The Ultimate Priority

 **I HOPE YOU HAVE ENJOYED** this meandering look at the wonderful challenge of raising boys. There is nothing to compare with the privilege of bringing precious children into the world and then guiding them step-by-step through their developmental years and on toward maturity.

Your task as a mother or father is to build a man out of the raw materials available implicitly in your delightful little boy. Construct him stone upon stone and precept upon precept. You must use the opportunities of these few short years to teach him your values and beliefs.

It is your job as parents to help your boys understand who God is and what He expects them to do. This teaching must begin very early in childhood. Even at three years of age, a child is capable of learning that the flowers, the sky, the birds, and even the rainbow are gifts from God's hand. He made these wonderful things, just as He created each one of us. The first Scripture children should learn is "God is love" (1 John 4:8). They should be taught to thank Him before eating their food and to ask for His help when they are hurt or scared.

Moses takes that responsibility a step further in Deuteronomy 6. He tells parents to talk about spiritual matters continually. "These commandments that I give you today are to be upon your hearts. Impress them on your children. Talk about them when you sit at home and when you walk along the road, when you lie down and when you get up. Tie them as symbols on your hands and bind them on your foreheads. Write them on the doorframes of your houses and on your gates" (Deuteronomy 6:6-9).

THE FIRST SCRIPTURE CHILDREN SHOULD LEARN IS "GOD IS LOVE." (1 JOHN 4:8)

If this passage means anything, it is that we are to give the greatest emphasis to the spiritual development of our children. Nothing even comes close to it in significance. The only way you can be with your precious children in the next life is to introduce them to Jesus Christ and His teachings, hopefully when they are young and impressionable. This is Task Number One in child rearing.

Not only is spiritual development of relevance to eternity, it is also critical to

the way your children will live out their days on this earth. Specifically, boys need to be well established in their faith in order to understand the meaning of good and evil. Teach them that good and evil are determined by the God of the universe and that He has given us an unchanging moral standard by which to live. He also offers forgiveness from sins, which boys (and girls) have good reason to need. Only with this understanding is a child being prepared to face the challenges that lie ahead.

Everything we do during these foundational child-rearing years should be bathed in prayer. There is not enough knowledge in the books—not in this one or any other—to secure the outcome of our parenting responsibility without divine help. That awesome realization hit me when our daughter, Danae, was only three years old. I recognized that having a Ph.D. in child development was not going to be enough to meet the challenges of parenthood. That is why Shirley and I began fasting and praying for Danae, and later for Ryan, almost every week from the time they were young. At least one of us bore that responsibility throughout their childhoods. In fact,

READY FOR TAKEOFF

The best time to begin preparing a child for the ultimate release is during the toddler years, before a relationship of dependence is established. However, the natural inclination of parents is to do the opposite. As Domeena Renshaw wrote,

> It may be easier for the child to feed himself; more untidy for him to dress himself; less clean when he attempts to bathe himself; less perfect for him to comb his hair; but unless his mother learns to sit on her hands and allow the child to cry and to try, she will overdo for the child, and independence will be delayed.[1]

This process of granting appropriate independence must continue throughout the elementary school years. Parents should permit their boys to go to summer camp even though it might be "safer" to keep them at home. Likewise, boys ought to be allowed to spend the night with their friends when invited. They should make their own beds, take care of their animals, and do their homework. In short, the parental purpose should be to grant increasing freedom and responsibility year by year, so that when the child gets beyond adult control, he will no longer need it.

When this assignment is handled properly, a high school senior should be virtually emancipated, even though he still lives with his parents. This was the case during my last year at home. When I was seventeen years of age, my parents tested my independence by going on a two-week trip and leaving me behind. They loaned me the family car and gave me permission to invite my (male) friends to spend the fourteen nights at our home. I remember being surprised by this move and the obvious risks they were taking. I could have thrown fourteen wild parties and wrecked the car and destroyed our residence. Frankly, I wondered if they were wise to give me that much latitude. I did behave responsibly (although our house suffered the effects of some typical adolescent horseplay).

After I was grown and married, I asked my mother why she took those risks—why she left me unsupervised for two weeks. She smiled and replied, "Because I knew in approximately one year you would be leaving for college, where you would have complete freedom with no one to tell you how to behave. And I wanted to expose you to that independence while you were still under my influence." Her intuitive wisdom was apparent once more. She was preparing me for the ultimate release, which often causes an overprotected young man to behave foolishly the moment he escapes the heavy hand of authority.[2]

[1] Domeena C. Renshaw, M.D., *The Hyperactive Child* (Chicago: Nelson-Hall Publishers, 1974), 63.
[2] Dr. James Dobson, *The Strong-Willed Child* (Wheaton, Ill.: Tyndale House Publishers, 1987), 217–218.

LETTING GO

Let me offer a couple of phrases that will guide your parenting efforts during the final era of childhood. The first is simply *Hold on with an open hand.* This implies that we still care about the outcome during early adulthood, but we must not clutch our children too tightly. Our grip must be relaxed. We should pray for them, love them, and even offer advice to them when it is sought. But the responsibility to make personal decisions must be borne by the next generation, and they must also accept the consequences of those choices.

Another phrase expressing a similar concept is *Hold them close and let them go.* Parents should be deeply involved in the lives of their young children, providing love and protection and authority. But when those children reach their late teens and early twenties, the cage door must be opened to the world outside. That is the most frightening time of parenthood, particularly for Christian mothers who care so deeply about the spiritual welfare of their families. How difficult it is to await an answer to the question, "Did I train them properly?" The tendency is to retain control in order to avoid hearing the wrong reply to that all-important question. Nevertheless, our sons are more likely to make proper choices when they do not have to rebel against our meddling interference.

My point is that love demands freedom. Why else did God give us the choice of either serving Him or rejecting His companionship? Why did He give Adam and Eve the option of eating forbidden fruit in the Garden of Eden, instead of forcing their obedience? Why didn't He just make men and women His slaves who were programmed to worship at His feet? The answers are found in the meaning of love. God gave us a free choice because there is no significance to love that knows no alternative. It is only when we come to Him because we hungrily seek His fellowship and communion that the relationship has any validity. Isn't this the meaning of Proverbs 8:17 (KJV), where He says, "I love them that love me; and those that seek me early shall find me"? That is the love that only freedom can produce. It cannot be demanded or coerced or required or programmed against our will. It can only be the product of a free choice that is honored even by the Almighty.

Adolescence is not an easy time of life for either generation; in fact, it can be downright terrifying. But the key to surviving this emotional experience is to lay the proper foundation and then face it with courage.[1]

[1]Dr. James Dobson, *The Strong-Willed Child* (Wheaton, Ill.: Tyndale House Publishers, 1987), 219–222.

Shirley continues that practice to this day. Our petition was the same through the early years: "Lord, give us the wisdom to raise the precious children whom you have loaned to us, and above all else, help us bring them to the feet of Jesus. This is more important to us than our health or our work or our finances. What we ask most fervently is that the circle be unbroken when we meet in heaven."

Again, prayer is the key to everything. I'm reminded of a story told by a rookie playing for the Chicago Bulls in the National Basketball Association. One night, the incomparable Michael Jordan scored sixty-six points, and the rookie was sent in for the last couple of minutes of the game. When the young man was interviewed by a reporter afterwards, he said, "Yeah, it was a great night.

Michael Jordan and I scored sixty-eight points."[12] That's the way I feel about parenting and prayer. We do all we can to score a few points, but the greater contribution is made by the Creator of children.

No matter how much you prepare, letting go is never easy. The late Erma Bombeck likened the parenting responsibility to flying a kite.[13] You start by trying to get the little craft off the ground, and sometimes you wonder if it's going to make it. You're running down the road as fast as you can with this awkward kite flapping in the wind behind you. Sometimes it crashes to the ground, so you tie on a longer tail and try it again. Suddenly it catches a little gust of wind and flies dangerously close to the power lines. Your heart is pounding as you survey the risk. But then without warning, the kite begins to tug on the string as it ascends into the sky. You release your grip little by little, and sooner than you expected, you come to the end of the twine. You stand on tiptoe holding the last inch between your thumb and forefinger. Then, reluctantly, you let go, permitting the kite to soar unfettered and independent in God's blue heaven.

It's an exhilarating and a terrifying moment, and one that was ordained from the day of your child's birth. With this final release, your task as a parent is finished. The kite is free, and so, for the first time in twenty years, are you.

My prayers will be with you as you discharge your God-given responsibility. Cherish every moment of it. And hug your kids while you can.

It's Tough on a Dog

By Jean W. Sawtell

It's tough on a dog when his boy grows up,

When he no longer romps and frolics like a pup.

It's tough on a dog when his boy gets old,

When they no longer cuddle on his bed when it's cold.

It's tough on a dog when his boy gets tall,

When he's off with the boys playing soccer and baseball.

They no longer paddle through the mud in the bog,

Hoping to find a stray turtle or frog.

They no longer run through the grass up to their knees,

Or roll in the piles of fresh fallen leaves.

It's tough on a dog when his boy gets tall,

When he's off to school, looking at girls in the hall.

It's tough on a dog when he has work to do,

When he forgets to play as he used to.

It's tough on a dog when instead of the woods or field or pond,

His boy becomes a man—and the man is gone.[14]

Endnotes

[1] "That Little Boy of Mine." Copyright © 1929 Forster Music Publisher, Inc. All rights reserved. Used by permission.

[2] John Attarian, "Let Boys Be Boys—Exploding Feminist Dogma," *The World and I,* 1 October 2000.

[3] William E. Schmidt, "For Town and Team, Honor Is Its Own Reward," *New York Times,* 22 May 1987, 1.

[4] Ibid.

[5] "Parent's Love Affects Child's Health," Reuters, 10 March 1997.

[6] Eric Wiggen, *The Gift of Grandparenting* (Wheaton, Ill.: Tyndale House Publishers, 2001), 27–28.

[7] Ibid., 29.

[8] Ibid., 33–34.

[9] Ibid., 69.

[10] Ibid., 162.

[11] Josh McDowell, "Helping Your Kids to Say No," *Focus on the Family,* 16 October 1987.

[12] Vice President Albert Gore, Jr. at Presidential Prayer Breakfast, 1995.

[13] Erma Bombeck, "Fragile Strings Join Parent, Child," *Arizona Republic*, 15 May 1977.

[14] Jean W. Sawtell, "It's Tough on a Dog." Copyright © 2000 by Jean Sawtell. All rights reserved.

Photography by John C. Russell, 7, 12, 18, 23, 25, 27, 29, 39, 41, 44, 48, 51, 53, 54–55, 56, 59, 61, 63, 65, 68, 70–71, 72, 77, 79, 81, 83, 85, 88, 91, 93, 94, 97, 102, 113, 114–115, 116, 119, 126, 129, 130, 133, 135.

Photography by Carl Yarbrough, v, viii, 2–3, 4, 8, 10, 15, 16–17, 21, 22, 30–31, 32, 36, 38, 47, 75, 86–87, 100–101, 107, 108, 111, 122, 124–125.